"Words of wisdom from an adult who is a lot like you! Bel... dreams. Don't be afraid of trying new things or let fear ho... on what could go right instead of what r..."

@NEURODIVERGENTREBEL (Christa Holmans)

"In a nutshell, 'My Pants' is a wonderful and engaging book that reminds us about the power of words and the diversity of children's learning styles. The children and families I support will go bananas for this one."

@CHILDLIFE_MOMENTOS (Kia Ferrer)

"I love this so much! I have so many students and other children in my life with sensory issues. I think OT's would love this book too."

@ABASPEECHBYROSE (Rosemarie Griffin)

Colie Creations

by Colie Creations, LLC
New Bern, NC

Copyright © 2021

All rights reserved.

ISBN: 978-0-9998011-1-6

MY PANTS

My name is Celana. I love pants. I can name every kind of pant that's ever been made. I really wish I could wear my cool baseball pants. Mom and Dad said I have to wait until next season.

That is all I needed to hear. They are my **softest** pants!

"She just needs more discipline," the doctor said. Mom grabbed my hand, and we left. Mom said the doctor was too big for her britches. That's silly. The doctor seemed skinny to me.

The next day was school picture day! Mom wanted me to wear a puffy dress, but it makes me

ITCH ITCH ITCH!

She let me wear my fancy pants instead!

I smiled as hard as I could. Before the camera flashed, I noticed a ketchup stain on the photographer's pants. The camera flashed and **Uh oh!**

I was sad when the picture arrived. Mom and dad said they were very proud of how still I sat for the picture. They made an appointment with another doctor to see why I was distracted.

A monster breaks into the office.

The lights are too bright!

Dad said we could sit in my closet and count my pants. That always makes me feel better. "You're such a smarty pants," he said. I am! Especially when I'm wearing my smarty pants.

The second doctor was different than the first doctor. He kept touching my arm.

"You just have to socialize her more," the doctor said.

Mom grabbed my hand and we left. Mom said the doctor got through school by the seat of his pants. That's silly. I don't think a person can sit that long.

The next day, I felt sad. I had so many thoughts running through my head. I cuddled with my favorite pairs of pants.

Mom came in and asked if she could hug me tight. I nodded. "Would you be willing to see one more doctor?" she asked. "We could whip out your **BEST** pair of pants."

"My **BEST** pair of pants?" I shouted. She told me to be quiet. **"That's right!"** I ran to my closet. I reached for the pants that were saved for very special occasions.

"Isn't this against the rules?" I asked. Mom said it was okay because she wears the pants in the family. That's silly. We all wear pants.

I showed up to the third doctor in my rainbow pants! These pants make me feel like I can do anything. **SHAKE SHAKE SHAKE!**

This doctor wore a big smile! He looked me in the eye and said it was nice to meet me. **"You don't have to look back at me if you don't want to,"** he said. That made me feel safe.

"Do you know what kind of pants I'm wearing?" he asked. It was a men's classic fit signature khaki cotton stretch pant with pleats. "Of course I do!" I shouted.

The doctor told my parents that I put my pants on one leg at a time just like other kids. I just learn things differently. He gave me a few tips to help calm the ants in my pants.

Stick to a routine. I like knowing what will happen next.

Some words and phrases have two different meanings. That's confusing. Did you know "ants in my pants" means nervous?

Lastly, have a safety place!

The next summer, mom and dad signed me up for baseball! I was finally able to wear the ants ON my pants! My coach lets me come early and count all of the balls.
1, 2, 3, 4, 5...

Name_____ Date_____

What do your favorite pants look like?

27

Name _____ Date _____

What is your safety place?

28

Name _____ Date _____

What does your silly face look like?

29

MY PANTS

Made in the USA
Columbia, SC
07 June 2021